CASTLES
AND
DUNGEONS

by John Hamilton

VISIT US AT

WWW.ABDOPUB.COM

Published by ABDO Publishing Company, 4940 Viking Drive, Suite 622, Edina, Minnesota 55435.
Copyright ©2006 by Abdo Consulting Group, Inc. International copyrights reserved in all countries.
No part of this book may be reproduced in any form without written permission from the publisher.
ABDO & Daughters™ is a trademark and logo of ABDO Publishing Company.

Printed in the United States.

Editor: Paul Joseph
Graphic Design: John Hamilton
Cover Design: TDI
Cover Illustration: *Magician Apprentice* detail ©1991 Don Maitz
Interior Photos and Illustrations: p 1 *Magician Apprentice* ©1991 Don Maitz; p 4 Tower of London,
©2005 John Hamilton; p 5 *Wizard's Approach* ©2003 Don Maitz; p 6 White Tower, ©2005 John
Hamilton; p 7 *Changeling Prince* ©1997 Don Maitz; p 8-9 *Prince Charming* ©1991 Don Maitz; p
10, Chichester Castle, courtesy Chichester District Museum; p 11 castle construction, Corbis; p 12
Knight at Sunset ©1991 Don Maitz; p 13 (top) stones & mortar, ©2005 John Hamilton; p 13 (bottom)
castle construction & defense, Corbis; p 14 Castel Nuovo, Corbis; p 15 Windsor Castle ©2005 John
Hamilton; p 16 staircase ©2005 John Hamilton; p 17 Dover Castle, Corbis; p 18 (top) chapel ©2005
John Hamilton; p 18 (bottom) curtain wall, Corbis; p 19 crenelated tower ©2005 John Hamilton; p
20 portcullis ©2005 John Hamilton; p 21 (top) arrow loop ©2005 John Hamilton; p 21 (bottom)
Bodiam Castle moat, Corbis; p 22 Bodiam Castle, Corbis; p 23 army attacks castle, Corbis; p 24 scene
from *Kingdom of Heaven*, Corbis; p 25 siege weapons, Corbis; p 26 wheel of fire, Corbis; p 27 *Magic
Dead* ©1999 Don Maitz; p 28 (top and bottom) Tower of London latrine, ©2005 John Hamilton; p 29
Chaucer reading, Mary Evans Picture Library.

Library of Congress Cataloging-in-Publication Data

Hamilton, John, 1959–
    Castles and dungeons / John Hamilton
        p. cm. — (Fantasy & folklore)
    Includes index.
    ISBN 1-59679-335-X
    1. Castles—Juvenile literature. 2. Prisons—Juvenile literature. 3. Fortification—Juvenile
literature. I. Title

    GT3550.H36 2005
    728.8'1—dc22

                                                        2005048312

CONTENTS

WHAT IS A CASTLE?

A castle is a large building that is heavily fortified. Its thick, high walls make it very hard to attack. It is a fortress where armies are based, but it is also much more. It is a residence where lords and ladies, knights and peasants, and kings and queens go about their daily lives. Most castles in Europe were built during the last half of the Middle Ages, from about 1000 to 1500 AD. Because they were both military bases and homes, castles tell us much about the people of the Middle Ages.

The Middle Ages were a time of feudalism, when local rulers called lords held great power. Lords were also often called barons, or princes, or sometimes knights. They all pledged loyalty to a king. In return, kings granted lords power to rule over large sections of land called fiefs. Most lords were very rich, and had regular soldiers plus mounted warriors called knights at their disposal. Lords built castles to house and protect their armies and horses, as well as their own families.

Facing page: Fantasy illustrator Don Maitz's *Wizard's Approach.*
Below: The Tower of London.

Castles were designed to strike fear into the local people so that lords could more easily rule over them. In this way, they were an offensive weapon used by conquering armies. People naturally didn't like their lands occupied by foreign armies. When massive castles were built, there wasn't much that an unarmed populace could do about it. Castles were often built on hills. They were a constant reminder to all who saw them that a lord was their ruler, and he had to be obeyed, or else.

Castles were also a defensive weapon, which is how most people think of them. They were safe places where people could flee in times of war. They were cleverly designed to protect and defend. Some could be quite huge, containing mini-cities within their walls. In the Middle Ages, castles and cathedrals were the biggest stone buildings in the land.

Castles were impressive symbols of power and wealth. In 1066, the Duke of Normandy, who was later called William the Conqueror, crossed the English Channel and invaded England. He won a great victory at the Battle of Hastings, and was crowned William I, King of England. He quickly took control of his new kingdom by building castles. He granted land to his loyal commanders and nobles, who were called the Normans. They then built immense fortresses in England, Ireland, Scotland, and Wales. England's famous Tower of London was built during this period. In this way, King William and his heirs established power, which kept the native people from regaining their land.

Facing page: Changeling Prince, by Don Maitz. *Below:* The Tower of London's White Tower. Construction was begun in the 11th century by William the Conqueror.

The Normans built castles almost everywhere in Britain. Hundreds of them still stand today. Castles were also very important in France, Germany, Scandinavia, Italy, and Spain. Central and Eastern Europe boasted many castles, including Bran Castle in Romania, home to Vlad Tepes, the 15th century ruler who inspired the legend of Dracula.

Byzantine and Muslim strongholds and fortifications in the Middle East were very well designed. These huge castles protected towns and trade routes, and were very effective as political and military centers. Knights who returned from the Crusades, especially in the 12th century, brought back many ideas, which were incorporated, into European castle designs.

Many extraordinary castles were also built in Japan in the 16th and 17th centuries. This was a time when local warlords held great power, much like the feudalism of medieval Europe. With so much unrest and civil war, warlords called Daimyos built huge castles for protection. These had large wooden towers, with overhanging roofs, surrounded by a series of stone walls and courtyards.

Castles finally began to lose their importance in Europe by the end of the 15th century. There was more peace in the land, and feudalism was gradually replaced by other kinds of government. Also, castles became vulnerable as gunpowder and firearms replaced swords and shields. Cannons were invented that could weaken or destroy castle walls.

As castles became less important, many were torn down. People used the stones to construct other buildings. Still, many survive today, a reminder of a time when castles were a source of power, fear, and protection over the land.

Right: Prince Charming, by Don Maitz.

BUILDING A CASTLE

One of the most important military purposes of a castle was to keep the enemy out, and let defenders shoot at attackers from behind a safe wall. The earliest castles in Europe were built in the 9th century. The Carolingian Empire, which covered most of today's France and Germany, was crumbling under the attack of barbarian raiders, including Vikings and Magyars. Local rulers defended their lands by building simple wooden forts. The builders often used natural defenses, like rivers or hills, to make the forts more difficult to attack.

The simplest castles were called *motte and bailey* castles. A motte was a large earthen mound, often man-made. Rock and dirt was piled up to a height between 10 and 100 feet (3 to 30 m). On top of the motte was built a wooden tower, which was sometimes put on sturdy stilts. In later years, the towers were made of stone so they could better withstand attacks.

Facing page: A page from a medieval manuscript showing a castle under construction. *Below:* Chichester Castle, an early motte and bailey castle in England.

Placed next to the motte was a large area enclosed by a shorter mound. This open area was the bailey, which was where most of the daily castle activities took place. The bailey was connected to the motte by wooden steps or ladders. The lord and his family lived in the tower on the motte. The tower was also used as a lookout post.

L es nes afet apareiller
E bien bozder e cheuiller
J ce fesoit mout biau afetr
E mout loz estoit necesseire
Q e qe sauenist ne qe non
C e estoit bien dzois e reison
Q e loz nes fussent atornees

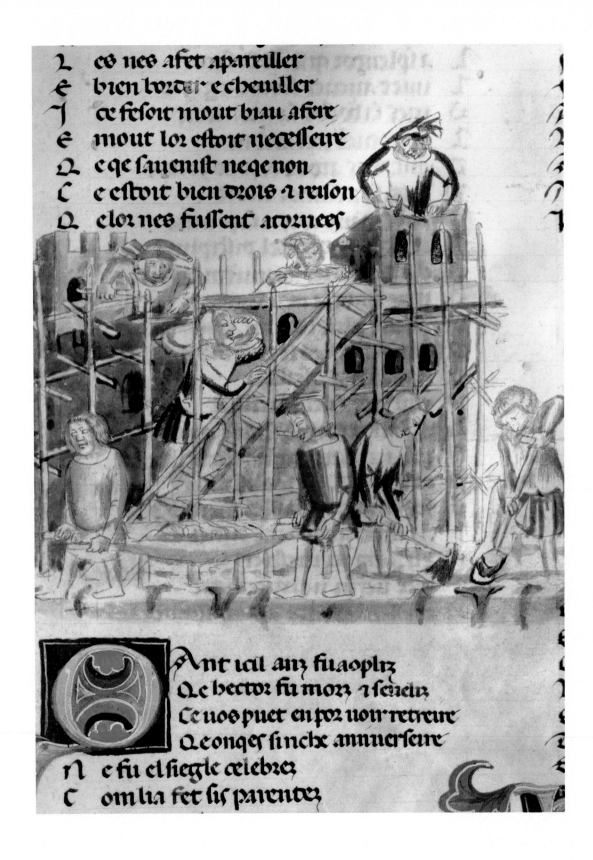

Ant icil anz fu aopliz
Q e hector fu mozt e seueliz
Ce nos puet en poz noir retreire
Q e onqes si riche anuerseire
N e fu el siegle celebrez
C om lia fet sis parentez

11

Motte and bailey castles weren't very sturdy. The wood rotted, and was easily set on fire by attacking armies. To make them stronger, castle builders began using stone. The earliest European stone castle was probably Doué-la-Fontaine, built around A.D. 950 in modern-day France. Stone castles were nearly fireproof, and could withstand most attacks by invaders.

Building stone castles was very hard work that took a long time. A rule-of-thumb was that each 10 feet (3.1 m) of height of a castle's walls took approximately one year of construction. Castle walls were very sturdy because they were so thick. Most castle walls were between 8 and 20 feet (2 to 6 m) thick.

Building stone castles took special skills, especially after the 12th century when they became very elaborate and complicated. Kings and lords spent fortunes building the most impressive castles in the land. Organizing such huge projects was very difficult. It took tremendous amounts of manpower, money, construction material, and time. An average castle took about 10 years to build. Some took much longer. Construction on Caernarfon Castle in north Wales lasted 45 years, and it was never completed!

Above: Stones and mortar used to build England's Tower of London.
Facing Page: Don Maitz's *Knight at Sunset.*
Below: A page from a medieval manuscript showing how a castle was built and defended.

Above: A page from a medieval manuscript shows workers building the Castel Nuovo of Naples, Italy.
Facing page: England's Windsor Castle started as a simple motte and bailey structure, then was rebuilt as the massive castle that stands today near London. Still in use by the Royal Family, it is the largest inhabited castle in the world.

The most important person in building a castle (not including the king) was the architect. He oversaw all the planning, including where the castle was placed, how it was designed, and what kind of material would be used.

Picking the right site was very important. The best sites had natural defenses, like rivers or steep cliffs, that could help defend the castle. A natural water supply, like a well, was also essential.

Stone was brought from quarries as close as possible to the construction site. Wood, for floors and ceilings, was brought from nearby forests. Other materials, like lead, iron, tin, or decorative stone, had to be mined and transported, which increased the cost of the castle.

Working under the architects were master masons, who oversaw the workforce and all the details that went into construction. Roughmasons worked under the master masons. They were the ones who actually built the walls. Freemasons were special stone carvers. They were more skilled, and did the work when fine detail was required.

Stone blocks were cut to the right size with large saws. The finer work was done using lump hammers and metal chisels, which came in several sizes. Metal squares were used to make sure the stone blocks were cut to precise 90-degree angles.

Many other kinds of workers were required to build castles. Smiths were hired to do metalwork, such as grills and the metal used on doors. Carpenters were also kept busy making things like doors and scaffolds.

The actual heavy work of building a castle was done by laborers who were servants of the local lord or king. They hauled heavy loads, mixed mortar for the stones, or dug ditches and post holes. Pay was very low by today's standards, but most workers were happy just to make a living.

PARTS OF A CASTLE

In Europe, starting in the 10th century, stone walls were used to replace the wood of older motte and bailey castles. The motte, the wooden tower built on a high earthen mound, was replaced by a tall stone tower called a *keep*, or *donjon*. It was the strongest part of the castle, where the lord and his defenders could retreat if the rest of the castle was captured by the enemy. Many Norman castles built in England featured a central keep. The Tower of London's White Tower is a good example of this.

Keeps had one defendable entrance. There were usually several floors, with rooms called garrisons to house soldiers, an armory to store weapons, and a great hall where the lord ate his meals. Other important people ate here also. Upstairs were bedrooms for the lord and his family. Down below were storerooms and the kitchen. In the tall corner towers, troops scanned the countryside, always on the lookout for enemy forces.

Spiral staircases made of stone wound through the towers of the keep. Staircases were cleverly designed to corkscrew around a central column. This saved precious space, and also had a defensive purpose. When going downstairs, the central column was always at a person's left side. Since most people are right handed, when a knight rushed downstairs to defend against invaders, he was free to slash his sword at the enemy. But when his opponent tried to swing his own sword, the central column got in the way. This made combat much more difficult for the attacker.

Facing page: England's Dover Castle was constructed in the 11th century.
Below: Staircases in castles, such as these in the Tower of London, wind downward counter-clockwise around a central column, which makes it easier to defend against attackers coming upstairs.

KEEP

INNER
CURTAIN

GATEHOUSE

TOWER

OUTER
CURTAIN

DRUM
TOWER

Keeps also included a chapel. Religion was an extremely important part of medieval life. Prayers were said before every meal, and before every battle. Knights believed they were fighting for good, under the guidance of God. Almost every castle had a chapel or other place of worship.

Surrounding the central keep was the *curtain wall*. It was the main defensive outer shell of the castle, made of thick, high stone walls. The curtain wall was built between a series of tall towers, which were used to observe and fight the enemy. The towers and curtain wall also were used as living quarters, and for storage.

Soldiers patrolled along the top of the curtain wall and the towers. The wall-walk was called an *allure*. The top of the walls had regularly spaced, squared openings that defenders could shoot arrows through. These defenses were called *battlements*, or *crenellations*. Battlements are a feature that most people recognize when they think of a castle. Sometimes cunning lords put battlements on weaker buildings to trick invaders into thinking the buildings were better defended than they really were.

The earliest castle towers were square-shaped. It was easier and cheaper to build them this way. Unfortunately, square-shaped towers were weaker, and easier for the enemy to topple down. One way they did this was to tunnel underground to one corner of the tower. This technique was called *undermining*. By digging away at the earth, as well as setting wood fires underneath, the foundation of the tower was weakened and the building sometimes crashed to the ground.

Because of the threat of undermining, castle builders began making their towers round-shaped. Even though they were more complicated and expensive to build, round towers were stronger. It was much harder for them to be pulled down by undermining. Also, cannon balls and rocks tossed by catapults often deflected harmlessly off round towers.

Below: A crenelated tower at England's Windsor Castle. Note the gargoyle waterspouts just below the crenelations at the top of the tower.

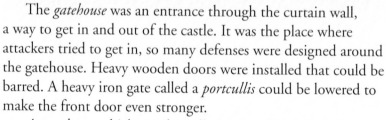

Above: A portcullis at an entryway to England's Tower of London.

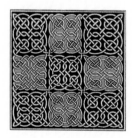

The *gatehouse* was an entrance through the curtain wall, a way to get in and out of the castle. It was the place where attackers tried to get in, so many defenses were designed around the gatehouse. Heavy wooden doors were installed that could be barred. A heavy iron gate called a *portcullis* could be lowered to make the front door even stronger.

Arrow loops, which are also called arrow slits or bow loops, were built into the curtain wall so archers could safely shoot at attackers. Arrow loops were normally a single vertical slit less than two inches (5 cm) wide and several feet in height. There were many different styles. In later years, a second horizontal slit was added, making the opening cross-shaped. This let archers cover a wider section of ground, and also allowed crossbows to fire through the slits.

A *barbican* was a tower built above the gatehouse that forced attackers into a narrow space where they were easier targets. Also, openings in the floor above, called *murder holes*, were used to drop stones or boiling liquids down on the heads of the enemy. Murder holes were also located in the tower that was built directly above the gatehouse. Usually boiling water was dumped on the enemy, but sometimes flaming oil was used, much to the invader's horror.

Castles often had rings of deep water around them called *moats*. This made castles even more difficult to attack. *Drawbridges*, operated by sets of chains and wheels, could be raised up, forcing attackers to swim the moat, where they might either drown or be easy targets for archers along the curtain wall. Sharpened sticks were also placed in the water to discourage invaders. Also, it was almost impossible to tunnel underneath a well-designed moat, so the risk of undermining was much less. It is a myth that alligators or crocodiles were kept in moats. Sometimes, however, moats were stocked with fish or eels to feed the people inside the castle.

Above: An arrow loop at the Tower of London.
Below: A moat surrounds England's Bodiam Castle.

21

In time, the design of castles changed. Tower castles ringed by a curtain wall were replaced by courtyard castles. These castles didn't need a central keep. The great hall and other rooms were built in the stone curtain walls, or in separate buildings inside a large central courtyard. Gardens were often planted in the courtyard to provide food for castle dwellers.

Facing page: Soldiers storm a castle gatehouse. *Below:* England's Bodiam Castle is an outstanding example of a courtyard castle.

Another design was called a concentric castle. They had at least two rings of defensive walls, with a large courtyard in the center. Attackers had to bust through two lines of defensive walls, and when they were in between, they came under attack by archers on both sides. Concentric castles became popular in the 13th century. Crusading knights returned from the Middle East with ideas borrowed from castles they had seen in that war-torn region.

The Siege

ttacking a castle was a difficult, time-consuming military operation called a *siege*. Enemy forces surrounded the castle and cut off critical supplies like food and water. They hoped that this blockade would force the castle residents to starve and give up. Sometimes, however, castles had better supplies than the armies surrounding them. Many sieges had to be called off after only a few months. Bad weather, sickness, or a lack of food in the surrounding countryside often forced invaders to retreat so they could feed and supply their hungry troops. But if castle residents ran out of food first, they would be forced to surrender. Secret tunnels were sometimes built so people in castles could smuggle in food and water.

Invaders launched direct assaults on castles in several ways. Battering rams were sometimes used to bash in the front entrances, but moats and drawbridges often made this impossible. Tunneling underground to weaken the castle walls, undermining, sometimes worked. But again, moats foiled this tactic. Also, castle defenders often dug their own tunnels. When the two sides met, there was fierce underground fighting.

Hundreds of archers shot arrows over the castle walls, hoping to hit people or livestock inside. Often, fire arrows were used to set any wooden structures inside ablaze.

Below: A curtain wall crumbles in this scene from the film *Kingdom of Heaven.*

For larger missiles, different kinds of catapults were used. *Ballistas* were like enormous crossbows, shooting huge metal arrows. *Mangonels* were a kind of catapult that used twisted ropes to fire a projectile. Sometimes diseased animals were launched into the castle in the hope of spreading plague. One grisly practice was to shoot the heads of slain defenders into the castle to cause panic and demoralize the troops inside. Castle

ARCHERS

SIEGE TOWER

BATTERING RAM

TREBUCHET

ARCHER

TREBUCHET

defenders used a variation of this tactic, putting enemy heads on wooden spikes and then mounting them on the battlements of the castle walls.

One way to batter down stone castle walls was to use a fearsome machine called a *trebuchet*. First used in the 12th century, trebuchets were large wooden catapults that used a long pivoting arm and a sling to hurl huge boulders.

When troops attacked a castle, they used swarms of ladders to try to climb the walls. This was made difficult by the castle defenders, who shot arrows, poured boiling water or flaming oil on them, or simply pushed the ladders off the walls. *Siege towers* were invented to protect the troops. These were gigantic wooden towers on wheels that were pushed right up against the castle. There were several floors inside that were connected by ladders. Siege towers gave the troops some protection before they leaped over the enemy's walls. Ancient Romans were the first to use siege towers.

Above: A diagram of a castle under attack, showing various kinds of siege weapons.

25

DUNGEONS

onjon is a French word that originally referred to the central tower, or keep, of a castle. As the centuries passed, the central keep became a less important structure, and was often converted to a storehouse, or a prison. In time, the word dungeon came to mean any kind of castle jail, especially one underground, where prisoners were tortured or put to death. England's Tower of London was famous as a castle that was used as a prison.

Being a prisoner in the Middle Ages was certainly unpleasant, and many castles did indeed have horrible dungeons, but torturing prisoners wasn't as widespread as most people believe. In fact, some prisoners, especially nobles, were treated relatively well. Many were free to come and go as they pleased, as long as a guard accompanied them.

Below: A "wheel of fire" was a torture device used to punish prisoners.

For most people, though, a castle prison could be a terrible place. Violence was a fact of life in the Middle Ages, and many prisoners were treated horribly as punishment, or to get information. Hot metal pokers, thumbscrews that dislocated fingers, and racks that stretched tendons and broke bones were all regularly used.

One especially terrible kind of prison was an *oubliette*. These were brutal places, even without physical torture. Someone sent to an oubliette probably never again saw the light of day. Oubliettes were stone holes in the ground, shaped like slender cylinders. Prisoners were tied to a rope and then slid through a trap door into these windowless pits. A metal grill was then slammed shut, plunging the prisoners into darkness. The door was too high up to reach, and there was barely room to squat down. Sometimes food was dropped into

the pit, but more often prisoners starved to death. Oubliettes were often built below ground level, and sometimes water seeped into them. It was almost impossible for forgotten prisoners to survive for long. In fact, the word oubliette comes from the French word *oublier*, which means, "to forget." Oubliettes were used throughout Europe and the Middle East, including the Bastille, in Paris, France. They were also used at the Black Tower of Rumeli Hirsari, in modern Turkey.

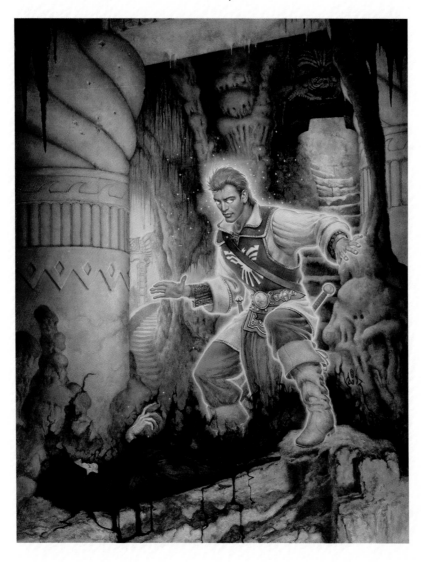

Left: Magic Dead, by Don Maitz.

LIFE IN A CASTLE

astles were busy places, and noisy and smelly. Even lords and nobles didn't have much luxury in a typical castle. The air and walls were usually cool and damp, even in the summer months. There wasn't much light, even during the day. At night the lord and his family kept warm by covering themselves with heavy blankets and fur, and sleeping near a central hearth or fireplace. Servants and soldiers had to shiver and make do with tiny lamps. Most servants slept on the floor wrapped in thin blankets, huddled next to each other to keep warm. Colorful tapestries often hung on castle walls to block the chill.

A castle was like a mini-community. It wasn't just nobles who lived there. Castles also housed soldiers and armourers, blacksmiths and gardeners, kitchen servants and falconers, not to mention livestock, especially horses. At dawn, the daily routine began. Servants lit the fires in the kitchens, meals were prepared, and trash was swept away. After a small breakfast of bread and drink, the lord and his family attended worship in the castle chapel. Afterward, the lord went about the business of managing his estate. To keep things running smoothly, he had to be a skilled politician, judge, and financial manager.

As the day progressed, peasants worked the land growing crops, and knights and soldiers prepared for future battles. While the lord ran the castle, servants and squires did chores to make sure all the nobles were happy. Dancers and singing minstrels entertained people. The lady of the castle spent her day supervising the servants, especially the kitchen staff and the spinners who kept everyone clothed.

Many of the things we take for granted today were nonexistent in medieval castles. For example, there was no plumbing, which meant no toilets to flush. Instead, most people used chamber pots,

Below: This latrine in the Tower of London's White Tower empties to the outside through a stone chute.

wooden buckets that had to be emptied and cleaned out by servants. Some castles, such as the Tower of London, had small rooms set aside to use as bathrooms, which back then were called latrines, privies, gongs, or necessariums. There was a simple stone seat that had a wooden cover with a hole in it. A stone shaft, called a latrine chute, emptied either into a pit in the castle basement, or directly into the moat. Sometimes iron bars were placed on the latrine chute to keep enemy soldiers from climbing up and invading the castle!

Life in a castle was not easy, despite what we see in movies or read about in fantasy books. Still, people have always been fascinated by castles. Seeing one, especially in person, brings a sense of wonder and awe. There's a part in all of us that wishes to live in a castle, even if only for a day.

Glossary

ALLURE

The walkway along the top of a defensive curtain wall surrounding a castle.

ARROW LOOP

Also called arrow slits or bow loops, these are narrow openings in a castle wall used by archers to shoot at invaders. Some are cross-shaped to let archers cover a wider section of ground, or to allow crossbows to shoot through the slit.

BALLISTA

A kind of catapult that looks like an enormous crossbow and shoots huge metal arrows.

BARBARIAN

A term used in the Middle Ages for anyone who didn't belong to one of the "great" civilizations such as the Greeks or Romans, or from the Christian kingdoms such as France or Britain.

BARBICAN

A defensive tower built above the gatehouse, the front entrance to a castle.

BATTLEMENTS

Regularly spaced, squared openings along the top of a castle's curtain wall, which archers could shoot through.

CHAMBER POT

Wooden or metal bucket that castle dwellers used as toilets and then emptied by hand into a drain or moat.

CURTAIN WALL

The main defensive outer shell of a castle, made of thick, high stone walls.

DONJON

Another word for "keep."

FIEF

A large section of land ruled by a king, lord, baron, or similar noble.

FOLKLORE

The unwritten traditions, legends, and customs of a culture. Folklore is usually passed down by word of mouth from generation to generation.

KEEP

A strong, centrally located tower where defenders could retreat if the rest of the castle was captured by enemy forces. The Tower of London's White Tower is a good example of a castle keep.

MEDIEVAL

Something from the Middle Ages.

MIDDLE AGES

In European history, a period defined by historians as between 476 A.D. and 1450 A.D.

NOBLE

Someone born into a class of people who have high social or political status. Sometimes ordinary people could be made nobles by doing something extraordinary, like fighting well on the battlefield. Usually, however, only people who are the sons or daughters of nobles get to be nobles themselves.

PORTCULLIS

A heavy iron gate that could be lowered in front of a wooden door to make it harder for invaders to enter a castle.

TAPESTRIES

A kind of cloth decoration, many of which are brilliantly colored with fine patterns or scenes, that hang on castle walls. In addition to being pretty to look at, tapestries helped keep out cold drafts that often blew through castle walls.

TREBUCHET

A kind of catapult that looks like a giant sling, used mainly to hurl huge boulders at castles to break down the walls.

UNDERMINING

Digging underground to weaken a castle's walls or towers.

INDEX